Plumbing Fixes Made Easy: Step-by-Step Instructions for Common Repairs

Ronin C. Turner

Fixes to Plumbing Every Homeowner Should Be Aware Of

Even though owning a home has many benefits, there will inevitably be repairs along the road, particularly when it comes to your plumbing system. Some problems, like repairing damaged sewer lines, should unquestionably be handled by a professional; thankfully, other solutions are simple do-it-yourself tasks that don't require specialized tools or knowledge. Find out the top five issues you're likely to run into and discover how to quickly fix them with these plumbing fixes.

STOP A TANK THAT IS SWEATING

After having a long, hot bath or a steamy shower, toilet tank condensation—the kind that drips into puddles on the floor—usually happens. When this occurs, condensation will accumulate because the restroom is hot and humid, but the water in the toilet tank is still cool (between 50 and 60 degrees Fahrenheit). Imagine a cold drink growing droplets outside the container on a hot summer day; that's what's happening to your toilet tank.

This plumbing repair includes installing an anti-condensation tank liner to stop the annoying issue. For less than $20, you can purchase them in kits at hardware and plumbing supply shops. Along with directions, the kit comes with a sizable sheet of flexible foam that you'll need to cut to size for the tank's interior. The liner may have a separate adhesive for installation or a peel-off backing, depending on the manufacturer. Before beginning, the tank must be drained and allowed to air dry. Puddles won't happen anymore once the liner is firmly in position (you might need to wait an extra day for the adhesive to dry). It will create an insulating barrier between the cold water and the outside tank.

TAKE A SINK TRAP OUT

Since most clogs form in the P, J, or S-shaped pipe that links to two other pipes beneath the basin, removing the sink trap is frequently the solution to basic plumbing issues like unclogging a sink. You might also discover something valuable caught in the trap if someone accidentally flushes a ring or other valuable down the toilet. To remove, clean, and replace a trap, follow these instructions.

1. Place a pan underneath the pipes under the sink to collect any leftover water that will drain out once the trap is removed.

2. Find the catch that joins the horizontal pipe known as the "waste arm" and the pipe that extends vertically from the sink drain. The trap has nuts holding it in position and is threaded on both ends. Telling family members not to use the water while you're working will suffice in place of turning off the sink's water supply.

3. Rotate the two screws holding the trap in place counterclockwise to loosen them. Most of the time, you can

do this with your hands, but if a nut is really stuck, use a flexible set of pliers; just take it slow so as not to damage the nut.

4. Pull the trap lower to release it. If it doesn't come off easily, carefully pull and wiggle it until it does. Let the water flow into the container you've set up under the sink.

5. Use an old butter knife to remove any stuck detritus from the trap. Next, take the trap outside and fully spray any sludge that may be coating the interior with water.

6. Reattach the now-clean trap by sliding it back into position and using your fingertips to turn the nuts holding it in place in a clockwise direction.

CAULK A VANITY SINK AGAIN

Your sink's initial plumber caulked the edge to prevent water from leaking between the basin and the countertop. The semi-solid waterproof sealant, however, has a tendency to deteriorate, harden, or crumble over time, allowing water to seep into the cupboard below, damaging stored items and encouraging the development of mold.

Purchase a small tube of 100% silicone caulk that is transparent or fits the countertop or sink if you want to re-caulk the area around the sink. the following procedures for the do-it-yourself sewage repair:

1. Use a plastic putty tool to remove the old caulk; a metal one risked damaging the countertop or sink.

2. Use a clean cloth dampened with denatured alcohol to wipe the seam between the sink and tabletop. Alcohol will eliminate any remaining detergent residue or grime.

3. Permit the region to fully dry.

4. To produce a uniform bead, apply a thin bead of caulk with a diameter of about 1/8" all the way around the sink. Maintain consistent pressure on the tube.

5. After gently running a fingertip along the caulk bead to smooth it into the crease and create a lovely, smooth groove, dampen it with water. You might need to repeatedly rewet your digit.

6. Prior to using the sink, let the caulk fully dry. The caulk tube lists the drying periods, which range from 12 to 24 hours.

TURN OFF A WATER HEATER TURN OFF

The efficiency of your water heater may be lowered by mineral deposit accumulation. You can prolong the life of your water heater and get more hot water by flushing it every six months. Although some models may differ slightly, the flushing instructions in the unit's manual are adequate for the majority of them.

1. Disconnect the water heater's power. Turn off the switch if it's electric. If it's gas, close the shut-off valve to switch the gas off.

2. Switch on another hot water faucet in your home, and let it flow until the water cools.

3. Place one end of a regular yard hose in a floor drain or a big bucket, and the other end into the drain outlet at the foot of the water heater.

4. Stop the water heater's water flow. The pipe that links the cold water supply to the top of the water heater has a shut-off valve on it.

5. Unscrew the drain valve on the drain outlet where the garden hose is attached using a flat-head screwdriver. Along with the water, mineral deposits and accumulated sludge will start to flow out of the hose. The water will be very hot, so take care not to get sprayed!

6. After the water stops draining out, screw the drain valve shut with a screwdriver, take the hose off, turn on the water heater's water supply, and then switch the electricity back on.

Contents

Understanding the Different Parts of a PlumbingSystem 1
Importance of Timely Plumbing Repairs 3
Must-Have Plumbing Tools 5
Toilet Repairs 22
Fixing Bathroom Shower and Tub Problems 37
Repairing Faulty Kitchen Taps, Faucets, and Sprayers 50
Sinks and Outdoor Faucet Repairs 57
Drainage Repairs for Tubs, Showers, Floor Drains, and More 68
Handling Pipe Repairs 79
Conclusion 89

Understanding the Different Parts of a Plumbing System

I know you are excited to learn how to do various plumbing repairs. However, before getting down to doing plumbing repairs like a pro, you must first understand how your plumbing system works.

Knowing how your home's plumbing system works will enable you to select the most suitable and safest pipes and fixtures and avoid plumbing catastrophes. This way, you can have a perfect plumbing system for years with appropriate maintenance and installation.

In addition, to diagnose plumbing issues when they arise, you must first know what your plumbing system comprises. Mostly, a plumbing system has the three components discussed below:

Pipes and Other Plumbing Fittings

Pipes and fittings are the skeleton or foundation of your home's plumbing system. Pipes help transport water from the main city line or water source to your home and the various locations where you need it.

On the other hand, fittings are the components that join one pipe to the next. They allow pipes to shift angles while still maximizing the space available within your ceilings, walls, and floors.

Most plumbing systems use two different pairs of pipes and fittings. The first pair transports cold water throughout the house, and the second pair is for hot water. Common materials used to make pipes include brass, lead, copper, or even PVC.

Plumbing Fixtures

As water moves from the supply pipes into your home, it requires a final destination. That is where the plumbing fixtures come in. Toilet sinks, kitchen sinks, bathtubs, showerheads, heaters, washing machines, dishwashers, and any other water-using appliances in your home are examples of fixtures.

Some of these items draw water from the pipes when needed, while others suck water from the pipes whenever turned on or pressed.

The Drainage System

Now:

After water enters your home and you use the shower or the dishwasher, where does the dirty water go? It goes through the drainage system to your septic system of the city sewer, depending on which waste disposal system you use. If your home didn't have a good drainage system, it would rapidly flood after washing the dishes or taking a few showers.

Each plumbing fixture has a drain that connects to the main drainage system through pipes. If you look below any of your sinks, you will see pipes that drain the dirty water away. That is a good example of a drain that is just a small part of the entire home's drainage system.

I hope you now understand how your home's plumbing system generally works. It's a lot more complicated than that, but these fundamentals should make it easy to understand the various plumbing repairs we will discuss later.

Why are plumbing repairs so important that we had to write a book about them? Read on to find out.

Importance of Timely Plumbing Repairs

Many homeowners may not realize the significance of a properly operating plumbing system until issues arise. While some plumbing issues result from forgetting to maintain your household plumbing, others arise due to the natural aging of plumbing components. Regardless of the cause of the plumbing issues, getting them fixed immediately is important because:

Prevents Unwanted Disruptions

When dealing with plumbing issues such as clogged drains and flooding toilets, you may need to turn off the water supply to your home until after resolving the problem. This may prevent you from using the toilet or carrying out daily domestic tasks like doing laundry or washing the dishes.

Timely plumbing repairs help keep routine household utilities and activities running smoothly by preventing unwanted disruptions.

Protects Your Home from Further Damage

Your home is unquestionably one of your most valuable assets. As such, you must do everything to maintain its value. If left unattended, plumbing issues such as leaky faucets and busted water pipes can lead to major water damage on your walls and floors. This can compromise structural stability, resulting in expensive building repairs.

By keeping water from accessing areas of the house that need to stay dry, early plumbing repairs are an effective approach to protect your home.

Protects Occupants from Mold Related Health Problems

Mold infestation is the most significant health risk of a leaky plumbing system. Asthmatics and people with allergic reactions suffer the most when there is mold in their homes.

Mold spores are practically everywhere, but they only grow on damp surfaces. Plumbing leaks can dampen your home's interior surfaces, providing the ideal habitat for mold to thrive. This puts your family's health in jeopardy.

It's important to repair plumbing leaks as soon as possible to keep your home dry and reduce the risk of mold infestation.

It Saves You Money

Apart from the money you save by doing plumbing repairs yourself instead of hiring someone, being timely with your repairs will save you money. This is because most plumbing issues get worse if left unattended. For example, a blocked drainpipe from the washing machine could cause the machine itself to malfunction. Therefore, to avoid unnecessary damages and expenses, it is always wise to do your repairs promptly.

By learning how to do plumbing repairs yourself, you can fix problems immediately after they arise instead of waiting for a plumber to come to your rescue.

Let's now move to the next chapter and see what tools you need to have in your home to fix common plumbing issues.

Must-Have Plumbing Tools

While fixing plumbing issues around your home may sound easy and fun, you will still need to handle the repairs with a lot of caution. Otherwise, you may end up with a dysfunctional plumbing system.

For that reason, homeowners need to have a set of plumbing tools at hand to ensure they can do each repair well. Remember, you cannot have the results of a pro if you do not have the right tools for the job.

Let's look at the various tools homeowners need for DIY plumbing repairs.

1. Plastic Tube Cutter

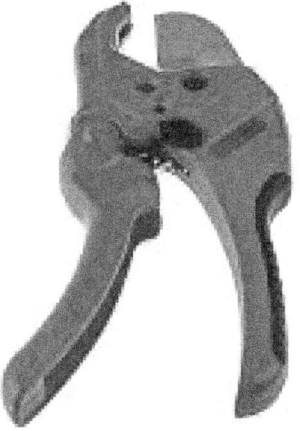

This tool helps plumbers cut through plastic tubes. The plastic tube cutter comes in various forms, but they always include a sharp blade that slices through plastic tubing. If you need to do plumbing repairs that involve cutting plastic water pipes, you will need this tool.

After applying pressure to a tube cutter, the sharp blade cuts through the plastic tubing. All you need to do is squeeze the two handles towards each other. Alternatively, you can roll the cutter's blade around your plastic pipe circularly, slicing farther through the plastic with each turn.

2. Metal Pipe Cutter

Normally, most tube cutters cut through plastic pipes. However, a plastic tube cutter will not do when you need to cut metallic pipes. Instead, you have to use a metal pipe cutter.

A pipe cutter operates by slowly slicing through the metal pipe and severing it with a sharp cutting wheel. The cutting disc slices through the pipe while the pipe cutter rotates in a circle around it. The cutter penetrates deeper into the pipe with each rotation until it cuts it completely.

3. Hack Saw

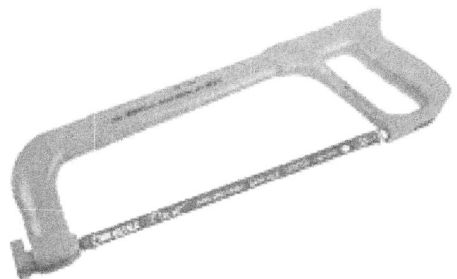

A hand-powered hacksaw helps plumbers cut steel pipes, bars, flanges, and similar fittings. This tool can also cut plastic pipes. The length of the saw's frame is extendable with a tightening nut or knob, which applies force on the blade and holds it in place. Moreover, you can set the blade to cut on the pushing and pulling stroke, with the push stroke being the most popular.

4. Hole Saw Kit

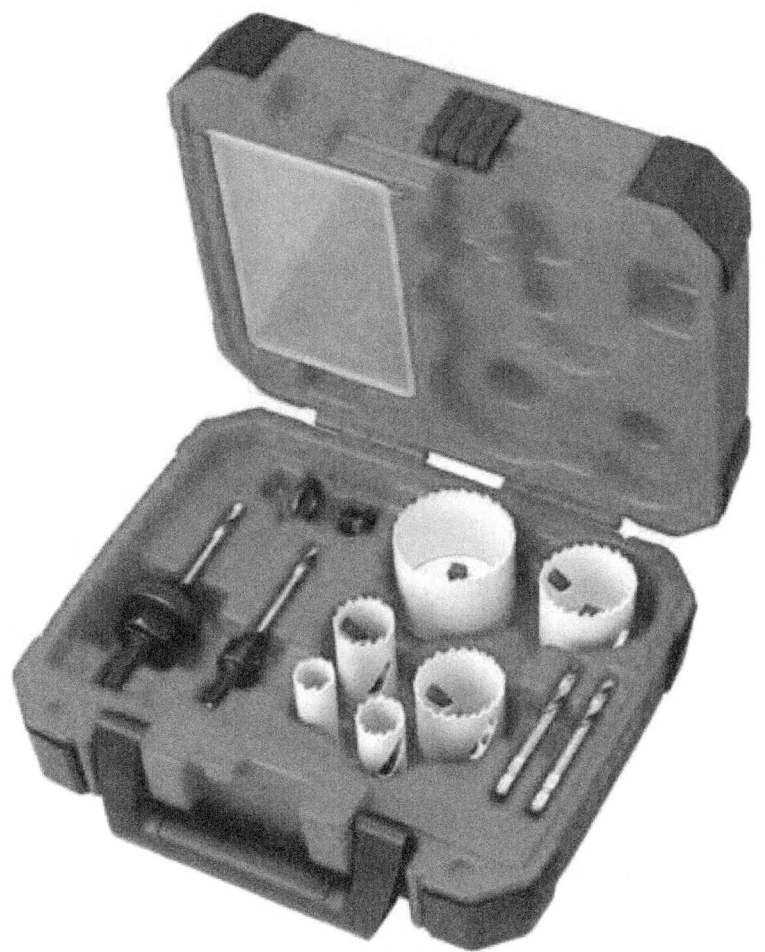

A hole-saw is a plumbing tool used to cut precisely round holes in different plumbing fittings. It can cut holes with far bigger diameters than typical drill bits and is much more effective than other drilling tools because it simply cuts out the outer line of the hole.

The hole saw needs to connect to a power drill that makes it spin at a fast speed. Consequently, the teeth of the saw cut into the chosen fitting as it revolves, removing a circular chunk (waste) as it goes.

5. Tube and Pipe Benders

A pipe or tube bender helps bend various plumbing pipes. For example, it is impossible to use a straight pipe when a pipe has to pass through various obstructions such as stairs. Thus, the pipe needs bending at different angles to pass up or down the stairs. Luckily with a pipe bender, this task should be easy to accomplish.

One of the greatest benefits of bending pipes is its capacity to eliminate the need to use pipe fittings to connect pipe pieces. Remember, it is better to use a bent, continuous pipe instead of cutting the pipe and connecting it using fittings because you eliminate any chances of water leakage.

6. Blowtorch

Blowtorches help plumbers solder and repair copper tubes and pipes. A plumber solders pipes by first heating them, then applying solder material, which melts in the heat. As the soldering material melts, it pours into the space between the pipes, forming a secure joint. Therefore, this tool is a must-have when you want to create tight joints on metallic pipes.

7. Plumbing Mole Grips

A mole grip —sometimes called a locking plier— is a handheld tool with adjustable jaws that lock around an object to keep it firmly in place. Mole grips are distinguished from typical pliers by their locking mechanism, which requires the user to keep them closed. Besides firmly holding pipes and other fixtures, mole grips can also help loosen various screws, bolts, and nuts.

8. Plumbing Pliers

These pliers have large handles and extendable jaws that lock in place at the touch of a button, making them the most commonly used tool in any plumber's toolbox. They're one of the most adaptable plumber's tools, with a wide range of opening sizes and the capacity to grab practically any shape. They can tighten or loosen almost anything.

It's good to have two plumbing pliers: one for stabilizing the pipe and the other for loosening and tightening. The 10" size should meet most of your plumbing needs, but it's good to have a variety of sizes.

9. Plumber's LED Flash Light

Some parts of your plumbing system may be in hidden and dark places, such as in the basement, on the ceiling, etc. Such places rarely have exposure to natural lighting. For this reason, it is important to have a flashlight to provide lighting when you're doing repairs in such places. While any regular flashlight can serve the purpose, it's best to have specific flashlights made for plumbers.

The plumber's flashlight should be small and compact, fitting into even the tiniest places. However, it should still provide intense illumination, just like larger, heavier flashlights.

Most of these flashlights come with flexible straps that help you position them anywhere and still rotate them at a 360-degree angle. More importantly, they are water-resistant to protect them from any splashes.

10. Pipe Threading Kit

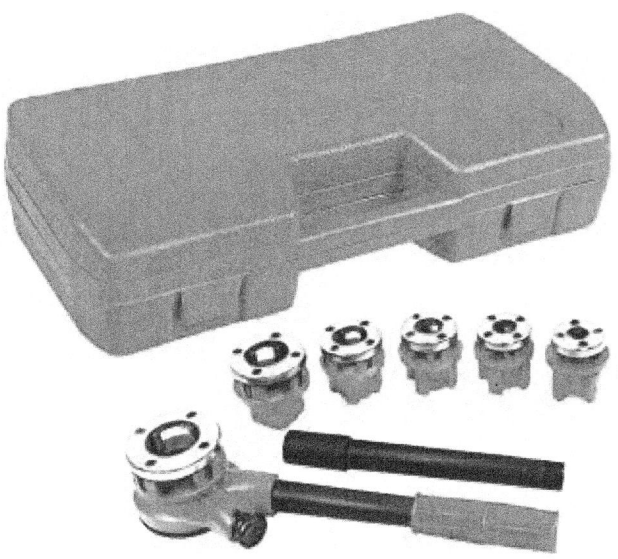

Pipe threaders are one of the most important tools. They help cut threads on the ends of tubes and pipes to create both female and male attachments with precision. They always come in handy when creating a joining two or more pipes.

If you require a pipe threader for your plumbing repair, you must select one that will complete the task efficiently. The tool comes in various sizes, ranging from heavy-duty, industrial-grade machines capable of threading wide pipes or more to small, hand-cranked threaders capable of threading thinner pipes.

Most pipe threaders are low-cost and designed to provide optimum output, even for the hardest pipes.

11. Pipe Wrench

A pipe wrench is a tool made of aluminum or steel used by plumbers to hold, loosen, or tighten circular pipes. This tool has a flat handle, a top hook jaw, and a lower heel jaw component. The lower jaw is movable up or down to match the diameter of the pipe. The jaw section comes with microscopic teeth or holes for holding round pipes when turned.

To help achieve the right grip amount and prevent damaging the pipe, there should be a 0.5-inch space between the rear of the hook jaw and the ground. Leaving this space also prevents you from hurting yourself or damaging the wrench.

12. Sink/Basin Wrench

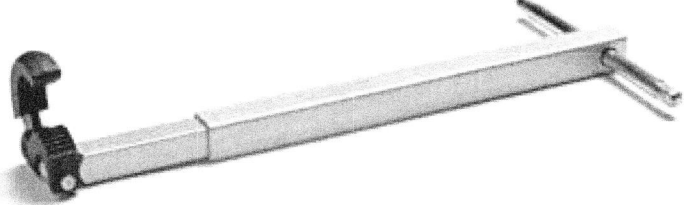

If you've ever tried tightening a loose nut on a regular spanner, you already know that it is an impossible mission. Luckily, there is the option of using a sink wrench, also called a basin wrench. This is a must-have tool for both professional and beginner plumbers.

It has a long handle and a revolving, self-adjusting, clutching head. Its main use is fastening or removing faucet tailpiece mounting bolts. The tool's design allows it to work in smaller spaces where other tools can't.

13. Plungers

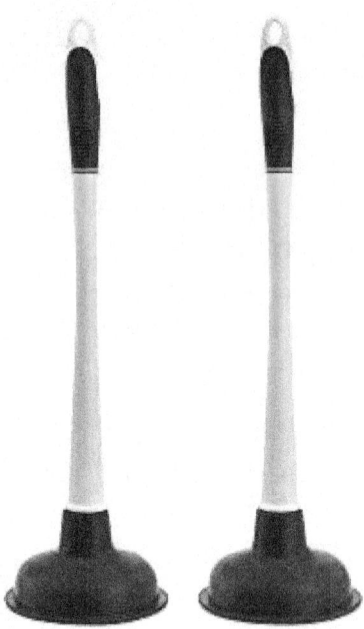

The plunger helps easily unclog blocked pipes and drains. This tool is simple-to-use, even if you don't know anything about plumbing. Normally, a plunger has a pole and a half-cup made of rubber attached to one end. A plunger is a tool every homeowner should have because it helps solve minor blockage issues in minutes.

Most homeowners use plungers to clear blocked sinks. However, did you know that you can also use this tool to unblock clogged toilets and shower drains? Yes, that's right, and this is why it is a must-have.

14. Hand Auger

A hand auger is a drain-clearing plumbing tool operated by hand. It comes with a 25-foot flexible steel wire used to unclog tubs, sinks, showers, and drain pipes. If the cause of the blockage is a solid but soft object, such as tree roots or glass fiber, the tool will split it open and allow the flow to continue.

In addition, the auger might snag a smaller, lighter clog, allowing you to pull it out. Some people use this tool to unblock clogged toilets even though it is not advisable because the auger may leave scratches on the toilet bowl.

15. Drain Camera

A sewage inspection camera helps determine whether sewer lines are obstructed, collapsed, or fractured. A drain camera is the easiest way to ensure that no tree roots have found their way into your home's sewage pipes. After all, sewer lines are smelly and disgusting to handle any other way.

The video camera captures the sewer's condition, exposing any fractures, tree roots, damaged lines, obstructions, and other issues. Therefore, if you suspect a blockage on your sewage pipes, use a camera to know exactly where the blockage is.

16. Plumbing Gloves

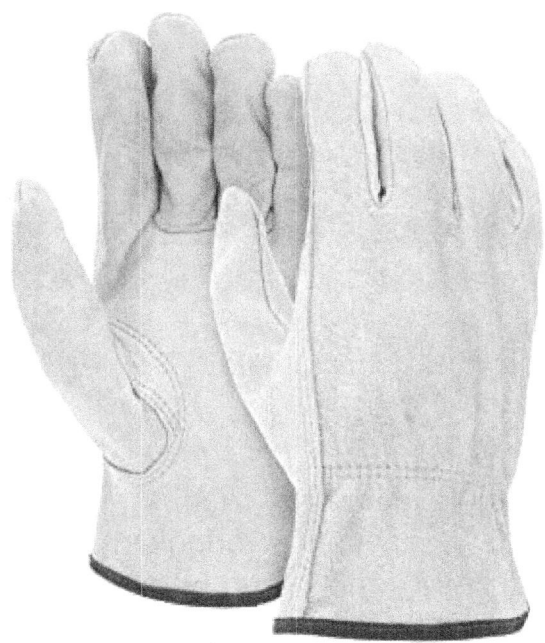

DIY plumbing repairs may sound simple, but you must protect yourself with gloves regardless. Working with pipes made of potentially ancient metals, such as copper exposes you to the risk of cuts from lacerated edges. In addition, handling hot pipes and using hand tools can be tough on your hands, necessitating tough plumber work gloves designed exclusively for plumbing repair tasks.

Although some plumbers avoid wearing gloves since they can impair accuracy, you need them to protect your hands from scrapes and burns. Disposable gloves may be useful for some repair tasks, but fabric gloves generally give more protection.

17. Safety Googles

Even as you do simple plumbing repairs around your home, it is always advisable to wear safety goggles to protect your eyes from debris, dirt, smoke, and other harmful chemicals. To put it another way, we wear safety glasses as a critical initial line of defense for our eyes which are sensitive body organs.

Thus, invest in a good pair of protective eyeglasses that do not fog. Safety goggles are a must-have, whether you're just cutting pipes or working in a dusty attic.

18. Tape Measure

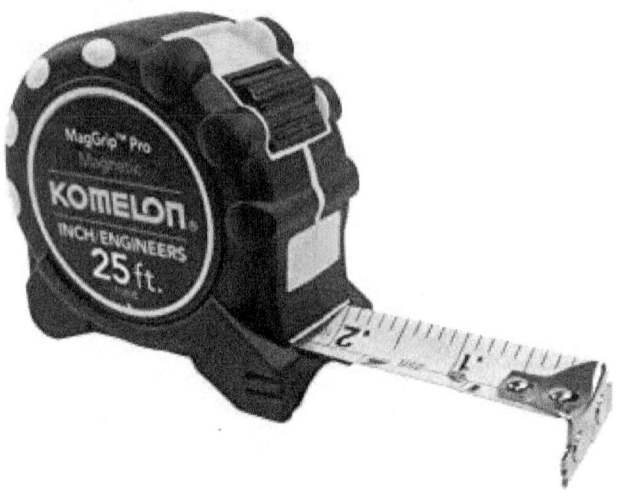

A basic measuring tape is the final plumbing tool needed by every plumber. When dealing with pipes, precise measurements are frequently required to ensure proper repairs in confined locations. A tape measure will help prevent costly mistakes caused by inaccurate length or distance measurements.

Remember, there is no end to the list of plumbing tools available today. However, this list is comprehensive, especially regarding the basics and the most used plumbing tools. More importantly, you do not have to buy all these tools immediately. You can always buy the tools you need for your current repair tasks and slowly grow your tool collection.

Now that we understand various plumbing tools and their uses, let's move on to the next chapter and look at the various repairs you can do using these tools.

Toilet Repairs

Some of the most common plumbing issues in a home revolve around the toilet. This chapter has everything you need to know about toilet plumbing repairs. Before we get into the repairs, let us first understand how a toilet works.

How Does a Flush Toilet Work?

The toilet bowl and the tank are the two primary components of a gravity-flush toilet. Let's start with the bowl, then go on to the tank.

Thanks to its simple yet brilliant design, the bowl is the most significant part of your toilet since it enables easy waste disposal via a siphon. When glancing at the side of the bowl, you'll notice a u-shaped part that links to the bowl and extends into the floor. This is the siphon, the component of the toilet bowl responsible for flushing stuff down into the sewer.

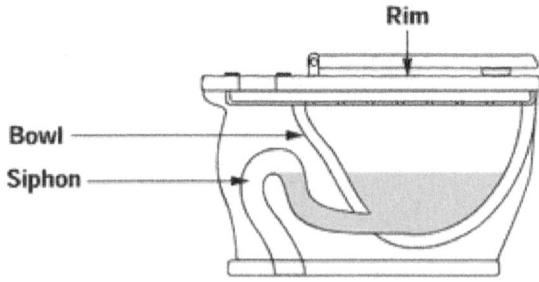

If you took physics in school, you might have learned about siphons. It is a term used to refer to any conduit that carries liquid upwards from a huge reservoir and then downwards by creating a vacuum. Gravity handles the rest after a significant amount of liquid pumps into the reservoir, propelling the water up the U shape and through the pipe. Because water molecules cling together, the siphon creates a vacuum that pushes the rest of the contents down that pipe as soon as water begins filling that U-shaped space.

Because of the siphon, even if you remove the tank from your toilet and only have the bowl section, you will still have a fully functional toilet. Notably, it wouldn't make much difference if you slowly poured a cup of water into the bowl. However, if you took a two-gallon pail of water and emptied it into the toilet bowl, gravity would take over and flush the water away.

The U-shape on a toilet bowl also acts as a seal, preventing gasses from the toilet bend and sewer from entering your home through the toilet. The flushing stops when air goes into the siphon, and the toilet bowl fills back up with water from the tank.

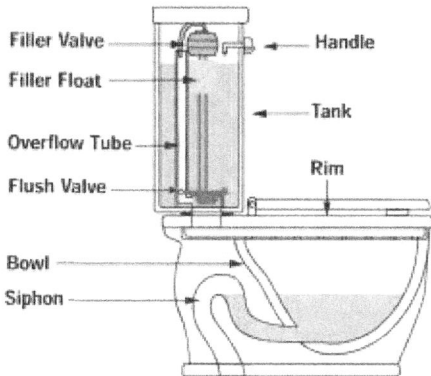

What is the role of the tank?

The tank functions similarly to a two-gallon bucket being poured into the bowl, only more precisely, and it accurately refills itself. The flushing process starts with a push of the tank's handle. Pressing the handle raises a lever joined to a chain.

This chain connects to a rubber flap at the tank's bottom while the rubber flapper attaches to the tank's seat. The thing is; the flapper is responsible for creating a seal between the toilet bowl and tank water. When you press the handle, it draws the rod up, breaching the seal and permitting the water in the tank to spill into the bowl, creating a flushing effect.

After every flush, the supply valve in the tank allows water in up to the fill valve, which starts filling the tank with water again. The flapper then returns to its original position, sealing the tank, thus preventing any further water from entering the bowl. The fill valve allows water to enter the tank until the float reaches the desired level, at which point it closes the fill valve.

To simplify all this, the toilet works in three steps:

The siphon triggers when the tank empties two gallons of water into the toilet bowl. It then pushes waste and water down into the drain and out to the sewer by gravity. The tank then refills with fresh water, ready for the next flush.

Now that you understand how a toilet works, let's look at how you can fix some of the most common toilet plumbing issues.

1. Fixing a Toilet That Does Not Flush Fully

One of the most typical toilet issues is needing to push the flush lever fully down to flush. The most probable cause of the problem is too much tension in the lifting chain connecting the flush lever to the flapper.

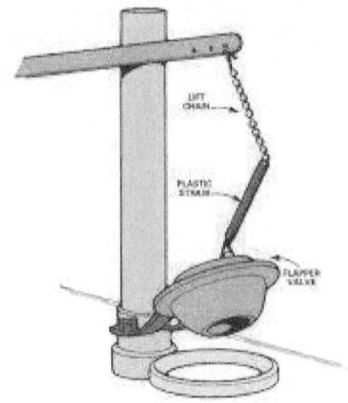

When the chain is too slack, it cannot lift the flap high enough to enable the required quantity of water to run down through the flush valve. As a result, the flapper closes prematurely, interrupting the flush. To fix this problem, follow the steps below:

- Examine the chain length to see if it needs adjusting: Look in the toilet tank for the chain. Adjust the length of the chain until only 1/2 inch of slack remains.

- Try flushing the toilet again: At this point, your toilet should completely flush with ease. However, if it still doesn't work, re-adjust the chain.

- See if the chain needs trimming: It's possible that the chain has stretched and become too long and is now dangling. This means you need to trim and shorten it using cutting pliers. Just make sure it does not hang down too far to interfere with any other toilet part. By so doing, your toilet should flush properly.

2. Stop Your Toilet from Running after a Flush

After a flush, water should stop flowing into the bowl. However, if your toilet is faulty, it will keep running, and water will continue to flow into the bowl indefinitely. This problem can be costly because it has the potential to waste many gallons of water if not addressed.

When such a problem occurs, it mostly means that the flapper has a problem because water will keep flowing down into the toilet bowl if the flapper does not properly reseal against the flush valve. After all, the water level never gets to the point required to cut off the water supply valve. Fortunately, you can fix this problem by following these simple steps:

- Check to see if the length of the lift chain needs reducing: Make sure the lift chain doesn't get stuck between the flapper and the flushing valve. If this is the case, water will flow into the toilet bowl after flushing. Reduce the length of the chain so that it does not get pinched under the flapper.
- Confirm if the flapper is properly aligned

Make sure the flapper is perfectly positioned in line with the flush valve opening, so it closes correctly. You might be able to stop the leakage by simply repositioning the flapper.

- See if the flapper needs to replacing: The flapper's rubber can never be able to stop the water flow into the toilet tank if it is old and damaged. In such a case, you have no choice but to change the flapper.

3. Tightening a Loose Toilet Seat

The frequent sitting, closing, and opening of the toilet seat gradually loosen the bolts that secure your toilet seat, resulting in a loose toilet seat. Fixing this one is simple. The only tool you need for the job is a screwdriver. In rare cases, you might need a pair of pliers and an adjustable wrench.

Remember, if the seat is in terrible condition, now is an excellent opportunity to buy and install a new one. However, if your toilet seat is fairly new but feels loose, follow the steps below to fix the problem.

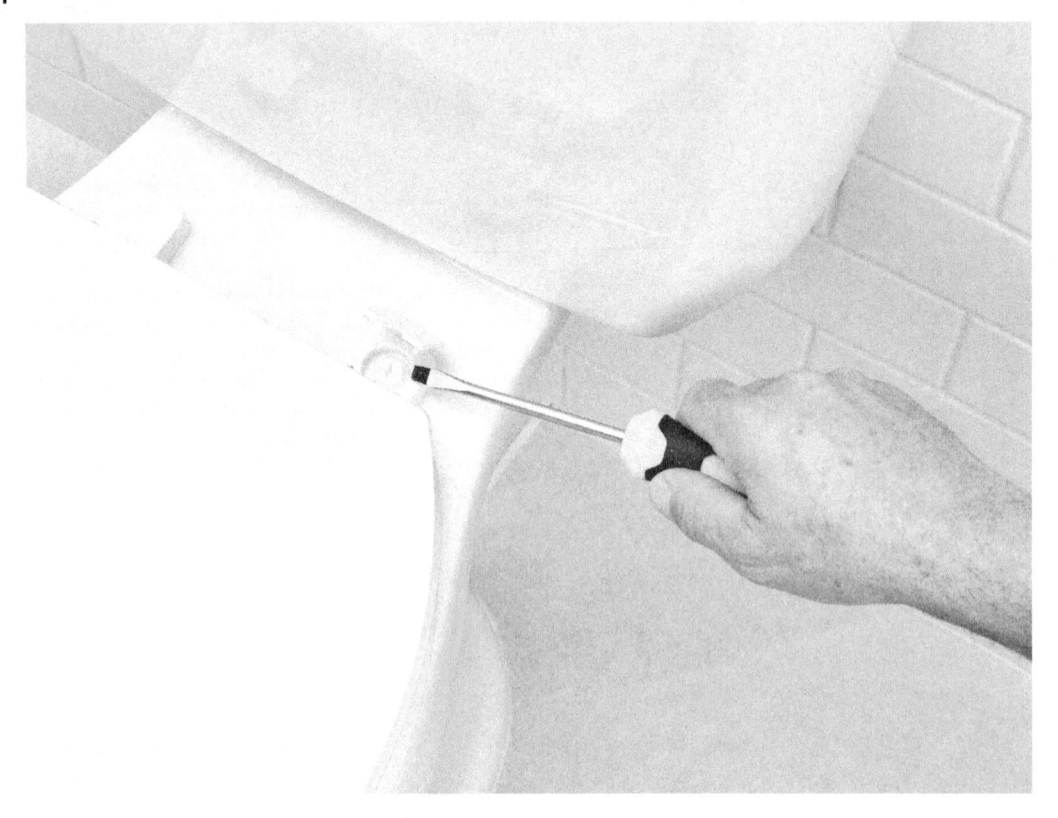

- Locate the Bolts: Some bolts are visible, but most are hidden by a plastic flap that clamps shut. To access the bolts that connect the seat to the top of your toilet bowl, peel these plastic covers open with a screwdriver.

- Tighten every bolt: If the nuts have grooved heads, fasten them with a screwdriver by twisting them clockwise until they are firm. Tighten the nuts on each side evenly to ensure your toilet seat is on a good level. If the bolt simply spins before tightening, grasp the nut screwed onto the bolt with pliers from under the toilet while stiffening the bolt with a screwdriver from above. Most toilet seats use steel screws, but if yours has plastic screws, be cautious not to break them or peel the threads.

- Tighten stubborn screws from the bottom up: You can adjust the attachment nut from the lower side if necessary. Turn the toilet seat nuts round from underneath the bowl until they are firm. Tightening these bolts is normally simplest with a ratchet wrench that has a deep socket, but an adjustable wrench can also work.

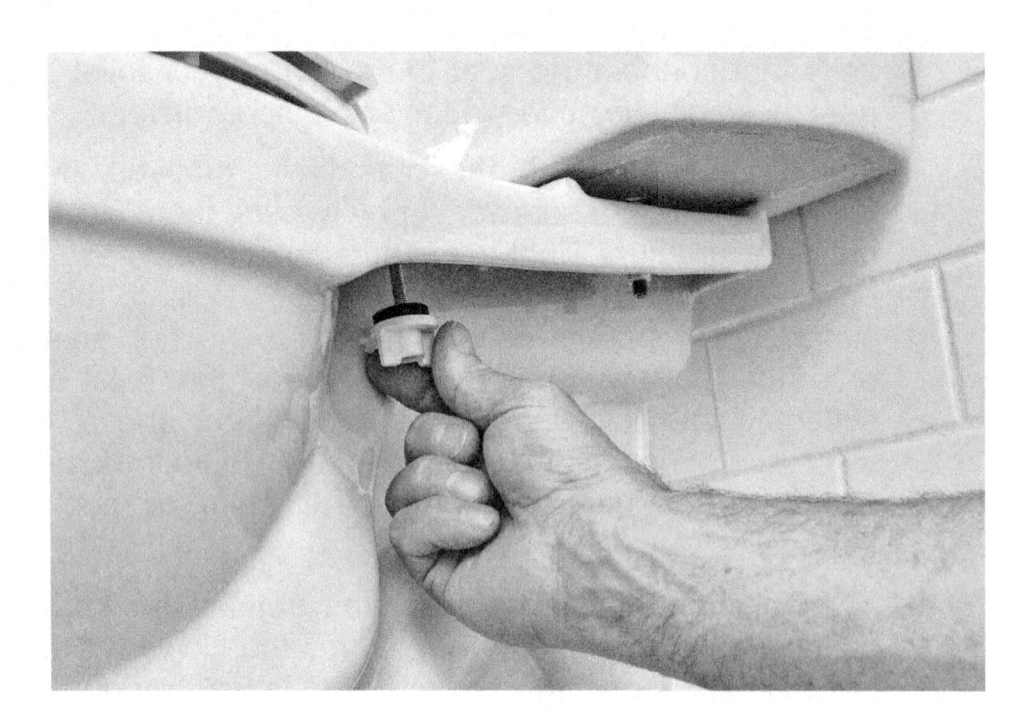

- If nothing works, replace the bolts: Sometimes, your current bolts may break or refuse to tighten no matter how hard you try. Luckily, you can find new bolts at a hardware store or home maintenance shop. Frozen bolts may require a sawing blade to remove because the blade is so narrow and can fit underneath the head of the bolt. That way, it can cut the bolt without scratching the ceramic on the bowl. After using new bolts, your loose toilet seat should feel firm, just like the first day after installation.

4. Fixing a Toilet that Fills Up Slowly

- Make sure the water supply shut-off is fully open

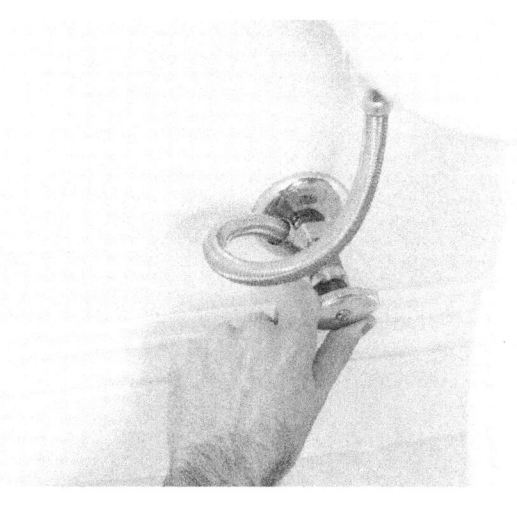

A toilet tank normally replenishes in three minutes— depending on your water pressure. If your toilet tank is taking a long time to fill or isn't filling, start with the toilet supply shut-off. For optimal water flow, make sure your water shut-off is fully open. Your slow-filling troubles may be caused by it not being fully open.

- Clean the pump and valve

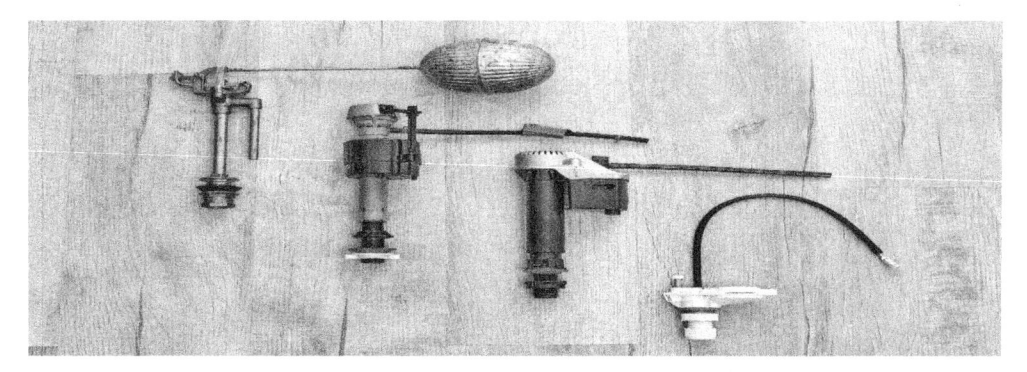

If you've tested the water supply and it's still not working, clean the pump and valve because debris could have accumulated over time, and a thorough cleaning may be necessary to resolve the problem. If there are mineral buildups on the outside of the fill valve, clean it with vinegar and a toothbrush. Wash the valves with warm water and soap once the buildup has come off. After that, give it a good rinse.

5. Plunging a Clogged Toilet

To know if your toilet is clogged, observe if it is draining waste very slowly. You will notice that the flush water partly fills the toilet bowl but does not rush out to wipe up the waste. The water level stays high for a while before draining to its normal level. Therefore, you may not notice that the toilet is blocked until you flush it.

Here is a simple process to fix this issue:

- Invest in the right plunger: Anyone can unclog approximately 90% of clogged toilets with the right toilet plunger. Make sure you purchase a plunger with a rubber, bell-shaped end with an extension flange. This is because it fits toilets better, allowing you to give the plunge more "oomph."
- Start Plunging

The simplest technique to clear "natural" blockages is to plunge—because a plunge may result in splashes, place towels around the toilet's base and relocate other objects to a safe, dry spot before plunging. Leaving a full toilet to sit for 20 or 30 minutes will often allow plenty of the water to drain to a more manageable level. The bowl needs to have enough water to cover the plunger fully.

To make a better closure with the entry at the bottom of the bowl, fold out the tail from inside the plunger. Pump the plunger a half-dozen times, then rest for a minute before repeating. Do this for 10 to 15 rounds.

If you can't create suction with the plunger after forcing enough water out of the bowl, fill the bowl with a regulated amount of water by raising up the flush valve in the reservoir. Plunge once more.

When you're sure the drain is clear, try a moderate flush, keeping your hand ready to block the flush valve if the water threatens to overflow. After the obstruction has cleared, flush the toilet with a five-gallon bucket of water to dislodge any remaining materials.

Now that you know how to fix the most common toilet problems, let's focus on fixing some of the most common bathtub and shower issues.

Fixing Bathroom Shower and Tub Problems

Nothing feels better than coming home to a warm bath after a long workday. However, you cannot enjoy such a simple pleasure if you have a malfunctioning shower or bathtub.

Let's look at some of the most common bathtub and shower issues and how you can fix them without calling a plumber.

6. Repairing a Leaky 3 Handle Tub or Shower Faucet

If your three-handle tub and shower faucets are leaking, don't bother calling a plumber since this is a job that almost anyone can do. Like any other faucet, a three-handle faucet might leak due to normal wear and tear or simply aging.

This type of faucet uses separate handles for cold and hot water, with a handle at the center diverting water flow from the bathtub faucet to the shower. You should be able to repair a leaking 3 handle bathroom faucet in the following few steps, despite its complicated appearance:

- First, turn off the water supply to the faucet: Before starting your repair, ensure you have your water supply turned off. If your faucet does not have any shut-offs for the bathroom, turn off the building's main supply water valves. Drain the faucets by turning the cold and hot faucet knobs to the open position after turning off the water supply. You can drain any remaining water by opening any taps located in lower positions. This will ensure you don't have even a single drop of water flowing to your faulty faucet.

- Uninstall your faucet to see the problem: Unplug the screws from the handles that control cold and hot water. Pull the handles away from the faucet stems with care. If the handles look rusty and are difficult to move, lubricate them using oil. If the handles remain stuck to the stem, detach them with any handle puller to avoid destroying them. Attach the pulling tool to the faucet handle and twist it until the stem releases the handle, turning anticlockwise to remove the escutcheon panel behind the handle—if it has one. If the escutcheon attaches to the plate by a screw, detach the screw and extract the escutcheon. With a flathead screwdriver, gently remove the escutcheon from the wall, exercising care not to deform it if it is stuck.

- Replace any worn-out parts: Turn the faucet handle anticlockwise with a shower valve socket wrench. Remove each valve stem's rubber and screw washer and tighten the screw after adding the new washer—use a flashlight to look into the valve. If the faucet seats are good as new, there is no need to fix them. However, you will need to replace the seats if they are worn out or scratched. Insert a seat wrench through each side of the valve and crank anticlockwise to remove the seats. Replace them with new ones and twist them clockwise to tighten them.

- Return your faucets and test for leaks: To reinstall your faucets, start by turning the stem clockwise into the valves, then fasten them with a tub socket wrench. After that, reinstall the faucet handles, which should be firm but not too tight. Reinstall the escutcheon plates and tighten the three faucet handles. Turn on your water supply to see if there are any leaks. If you don't see any leaks, go ahead and take a shower or a bath and reward yourself for a job well done.

7. Repairing a Faulty Shower Diverter Valve

The work of a shower diverter valve is to redirect water flow from the tub to the showerhead and vice versa. After use for a long time, this valve is prone to wear and tear, causing it to malfunction or start leaking. To fix this problem, follow these simple steps:

- Shut off the water supply and uninstall the shower diverter valve

Before detaching the handles, make sure the water supply to the faucet is off. Using a screwdriver, pry the ornamental top from the valve handle. If the escutcheon gets in the way of using your deep-socket wrench, it may be essential to remove it. The Shower Valve Socket should be threaded over the diverting valve stem and tightened over the bonnet screw. Go ahead and uninstall it.

- Inspect the seat washer and screw

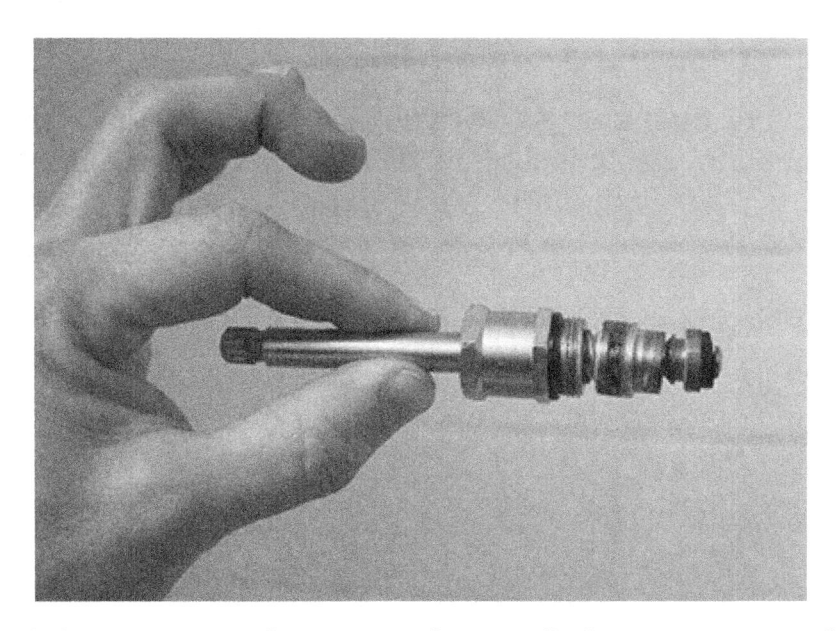

To reveal the screw and seat washer, pull the stem away from the bathroom wall. Examine the inner side of the tube to ensure that no O-rings or washers from the old valve have gotten stuck there. If you find any, pull them out and throw them away. They could be the source of all your diverter valve problems.

- Replace the seat washer if need be: If you have a worn-out seat washer, replace it with a new one coated with heat-resistant faucet grease. Use the suitable seat washer size and shape, then press it tightly into the stem's retainer.
- Reassemble the valve and test: You can reassemble the shower knobs and test if the diverter valve is working well.

8. Fixing a Clogged Shower Head

It can be very frustrating when you are just trying to enjoy a cold shower, but the water is barely coming out of your showerhead. Don't worry. This problem is easy to fix in just a few steps listed below:

- Clean the showerhead

Sometimes, your showerhead has low water flow because of clogging. That means you need to clean it and make sure all its nozzles are open. You can do this by rubbing the nozzles with a toothbrush.

Alternatively, wrap a plastic bag full of water mixed with vinegar at the ratio of 1:1 around the showerhead, as shown in the photo above, to clean it.

If that doesn't work, unplug the showerhead using your hands or an adjustable wrench and extract the filter screen.

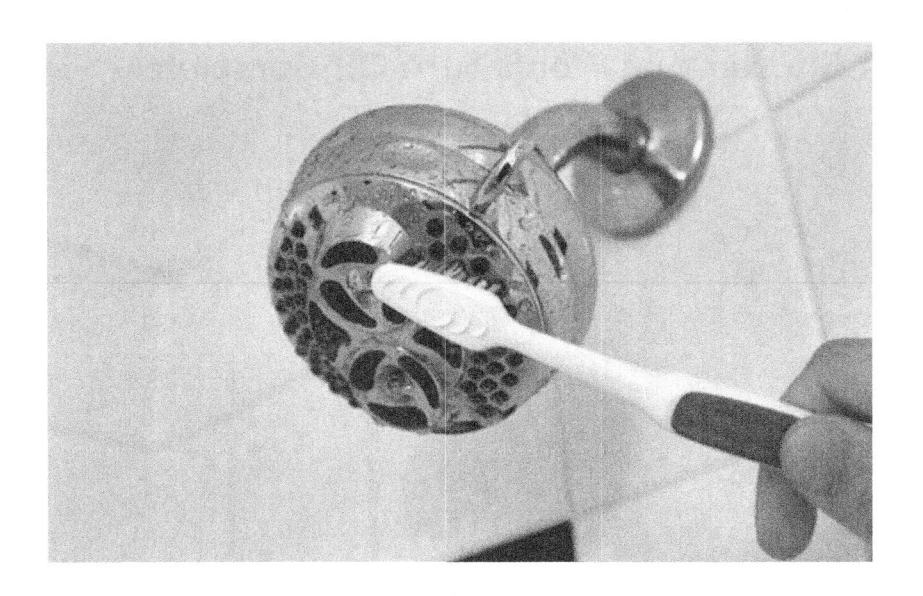

- Clean the filter screen: Normally, the filter screen is a metal mesh disc covered with a rubber gasket and is located at the point where the showerhead connects with the water supply pipe. Its purpose is to filter out any dirt before the water gets to the showerhead. Remove the screen with tweezers and clean it thoroughly.

- Reinstall the showerhead: After cleaning everything thoroughly, put back the showerhead by hand. You can use an adjustable wrench to tighten it at the joint. Turn on the water and test to see if the water flow is good.

9. Repairing a Shower that Won't Turn Off Completely

After using your shower many times, you may reach a point where water is left leaking from the shower even after you turn it off. This simply means that your shower valve washer seat has malfunctioned. To repair it, follow these steps:

- Turn off the water supply: Start by turning any water supply to the shower. Depending on your home's plumbing system design, you can use the shut-off valve in the bathroom or the main house shut-off.

- Remove the faucet handle: In the narrow spot along the rim of the faucet handle pushbutton, insert the blade of a flat-headed screwdriver. Remove the button from the handle with the screwdriver to reveal the screw. Pull the bathroom faucet handle away from the shower stem by removing the uncovered screw. Pull the stem from the wall by turning it anticlockwise with a shower stem socket.

- Extract the worn-out valve washer seat: Simply enter your seat wrench into the stem aperture. Remove the broken valve washer seat by turning the wrench anticlockwise.

- Install a new valve washer seat: First, apply a lubricant to the new seat's threads before placing them, then insert the seat of the wrench into the opening in the stem. Tighten the replacement valve washer seat by turning the wrench clockwise.

- Put everything back and test: Place the stem back in the shower wall's stem opening. Tighten the shower stem by turning it clockwise using the shower stem socket. Use the handle to cover the stem and fasten it with the nuts you took out before. Reattach the button to the handle and switch on the water supply in your shower. Your shower should now close properly.

10. Fixing a Hand Shower That Leaks After Turning On Water

A leaking shower head is usually straightforward to repair. However, before you begin, you must first determine the root of the problem, which is straightforward enough.

If your showerhead leaks after turning on the water, the rubber washer or the O-ring within the showerhead where it attaches to the hose is most likely to blame. If it leaks even when the water is turned off, the issue is most likely with the cartridge hidden behind the handle on the wall.

First, let's look at how to fix a hand shower that only leaks when the water is running. Simply follow these simple steps:

- Detach the hand shower: You most likely have a malfunctioning washer if your shower head leaks from the intersection where the supply line feeds into the hand shower head. Pull the showerhead off by pressing the release button. However, if your showerhead does not have a release button, simply rotate the nut holding the showerhead using a piece of cloth for a tight grip.

- Remove the old washer and replace it with a new one: You will see a rubber washer inside the entrance of the showerhead. Remove it and replace it with a new one.
- Reassemble the showerhead and place it back to test.

If the leak was because of a worn-out washer, your shower should now be as good as new.

11. Fixing a Hand Shower that Leaks With The Water Turned Off

If your hand shower leaks even when the main shower is turned off, the cartridge is faulty. The cartridge is a regulating device behind the handle responsible for opening and shutting off the water supply to the hand shower head. To fix the problem, replace this cartridge with a new one by following these few steps:

- Shut off the water supply: You can do this from the bathroom or the house's main supply.

- Remove the handle: Use a screwdriver to loosen the handle screws and remove the entire handle. Remember to put the drain stopper on to ensure that if any screws fall on the ground, they will not roll down the drain.

- Extract the Cartridge: Now that the handle is off, the cartridge should be visible. It is normally a pin popping out of a round assembly. Remove it gently, but if it does not come out easily, use channel locks or pliers to twist it out. Remove any dirt or debris in that space.

- Insert the new cartridge and test: Take your new cartridge and place it with the pin looking back just like the old cartridge had been positioned. Reassemble the handle and turn on the water supply for testing. You should now have your hand shower well repaired with zero leaks.

Now that we have completed the most common bathtub and shower repairs, let's move on to the next chapter and see how you should fix your sprayer plumbing issues.

Repairing Faulty Kitchen Taps, Faucets, and Sprayers

Everyone loves to have a fully functional kitchen—that's why we invest in sprayers to make cleaning and other kitchen chores easier.

Unfortunately, these sprayers are very prone to wear and tear because of the constant movement needed when using them. For that reason, they tend to keep malfunctioning.

Let's look at how you can fix some of your sprayer issues without paying a plumber.

12. Repairing a Pullout Faucet That Won't Retract

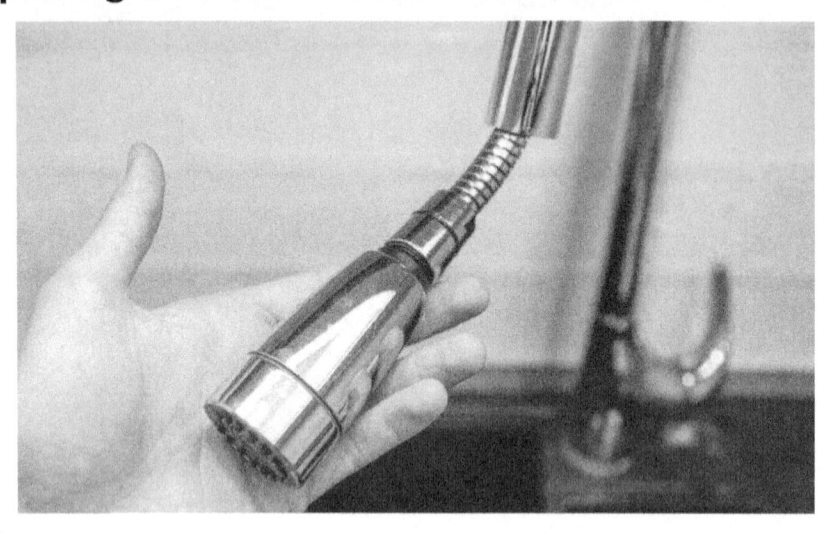

When your pullout sprayer refuses to retract, you'll have to push it back physically, a tedious and unpleasant task. Pullout hoses have an extra weight connected to them, causing them to retract because of gravity. Therefore, when they fail to retract, it could be that this weight is off or that the spraying hose is old. To fix the problem, follow the steps below:

- Check if the hose is still attached to the faucet: Look under the sink to see if the sprayer hose still connects to the faucet. If the hose is separated, you may easily reposition it by shifting the weight up or down until you have the hose correctly reinstalled.

- Untangle the hose: If you discover your faucet's spraying hose or tubing has become tangled with the water tube valve, you can untangle it by rotating the valve down and up. This will also assist the faucet in starting to retract.
- Fix the Weight

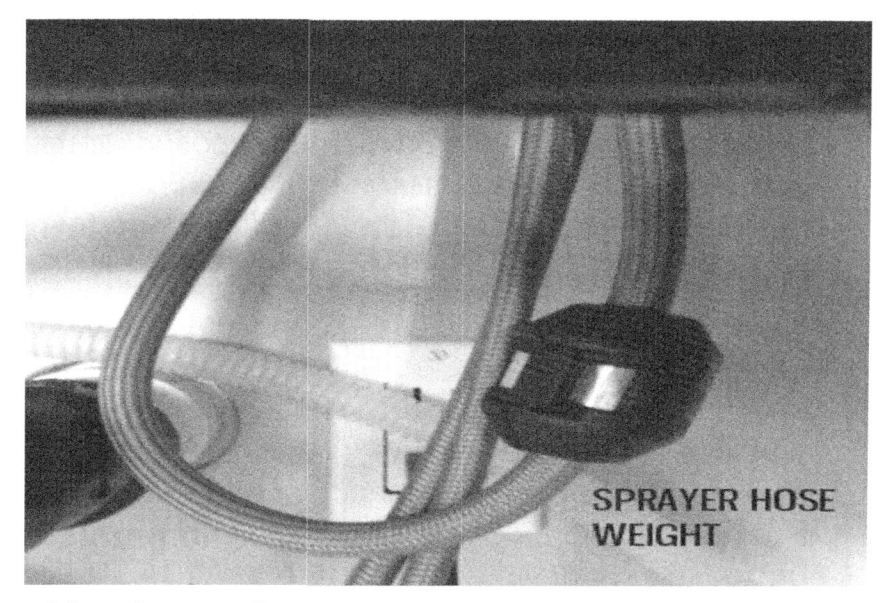

SPRAYER HOSE WEIGHT

If the problem is your faucet's weight, simply buy some faucet weight and replace it using a screwdriver.

13. Repairing a Clogged Diverter Valve

A diverter valve helps water flow to your sprayer after turning on your faucet. Unfortunately, after using the sprayer for long, the diverter valve gets clogged with water minerals and other particles blocking water from getting to the sprayer. To fix this problem, follow these easy steps:

- Turn the water off and unscrew the handle: Turn off the water valves before using a flathead screwdriver to unscrew the main handle screw. After that, flip the cap anticlockwise to expose the faucet's cap and detach the handle.

- Detach the spout: Remove the exposed cam to gain access to the tap ball assembly, which you should also remove. Then detach the spout by rotating it severally until it becomes loose and comes off.

- Remove the diverter, clean it, and put everything back: Locate the diverter in the front end of the faucet's handle and unscrew it so you may clear away the blocked dirt particles with vinegar. After washing and drying the diverter, return it to its original place in the kitchen faucet. Put everything back as it was and enjoy using an unclogged sprayer.

14. Fixing Low Water Pressure in the kitchen

While low water pressure has many causes, a clogged aerator is the most common cause, which often happens when you use hard water in the kitchen—it leaves behind mineral deposits that clog the aerator. Fortunately, this problem is easy to fix if you follow the steps below:

- Open the spout to access the aerator: You'll need to untwist the aerator from the side of the main vent using your hands to move it in a clockwise direction. If the aerator becomes stuck and is difficult to turn, use a set of pliers to pry it open. However, take care not to scratch the surface with a firm hold on the pliers by wrapping masking tape around the pliers' jaws. Having opened the spout, you can use your finger or a screwdriver to check if any aerator parts are stuck inside it.

- Remove any stuck particles and minerals: Using your screwdriver, pry out any materials trapped inside the spout, then clear away any remaining debris. Using any tiny pointy tool, disassemble every section of your aerator. Before disassembling any part, make a mental note of how where everything goes. You can take photographs to use as a reference later.

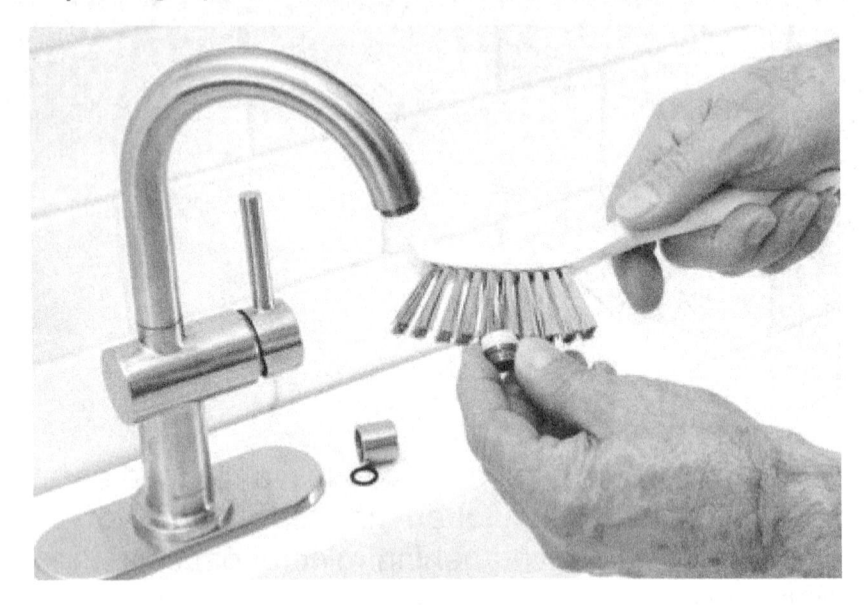

- Clean every part of the aerator in vinegar before putting everything back: Clean all the parts by dipping them in vinegar or wiping them down with a moist dipped-in-vinegar cloth. This aids in the dissolution of all mineral formations. Finally, rotate the aerator anticlockwise to rinse, reassemble, and reattach it to the spout. Make sure it's as tight as you can get it with your hands.

15. Fixing a Leaky Kitchen Tap or Sprayer

If the head of your kitchen tap or sprayer is leaky, you have no other option but to replace it. Luckily, it is an easy task that you can complete by following the easy steps below:

- Start by cutting off the water supply to your kitchen sink first: You can do this by turning off the water valves found beneath the sink.

- Remove the faucet head together with the C-clip: After cutting off the water supply, use your pocket screwdriver to remove the old faucet head, exposing the C-clip and removing it.

- Install a new faucet head: You'll need to install the new faucet head after removing the old C-clip. First, use a washer to secure the new C-clip. After that, you may use your flat head screwdriver to install the new head by placing it like your old faucet head.

- Always keep your faucet head clean: After fitting a new faucet head, unscrew it now and again to clear out the dirt accumulated on it. That way, you'll improve its performance and reduce the chances of sudden leaks.

Let's now look at repairing common sink and faucet problems:

Sinks and Outdoor Faucet Repairs

Another set of common plumbing issues in a home revolves around sinks, taps, and regular faucets. You could have sinks and taps in different parts of your house, such as the kitchen, bathroom, dining area, outdoor areas, etc. The more sinks and taps you have, the more plumbing issues you'll face.

Let's look at how you can do some of these repairs.

16. How to Fix a Loose Sink

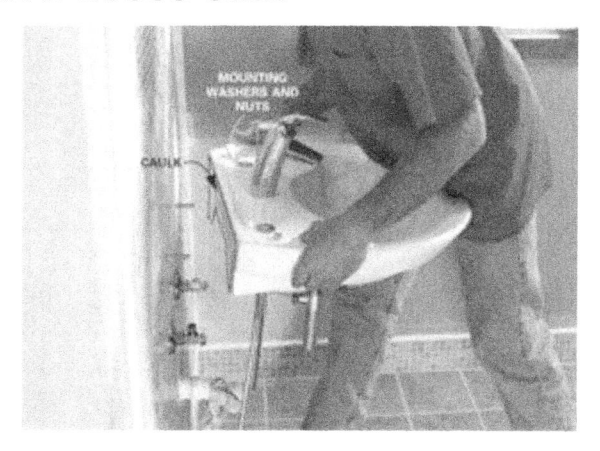

After using your sinks for a long time, you might notice some of them feeling loose. They start to shake and wobble every time you use them. To make your sink firm again, follow the steps below:

- Inspect to see if the sink is in good condition: Sometimes, a sink starts to feel loose after breaking. In such a case, you will have no choice but to replace it with a new one. However, if you inspect the sink and find that it is in good condition, you will only need to do a few repairs to fix your problem.

- Look for loose screws and attachment hardware: Sinks usually attach to the wall using screws and other attachment hardware. If you find that the screws are loose, use a screwdriver to tighten them. Remember, it all depends on the type of sink you have and how it was installed. If metal rods support your sink, check to see if the metal rods are loose or rusted, and replace them to make your sink firm again.

17. How to Fix a Leaky Sink

First, study the image below and see the different parts of a sink to understand the repair process better.

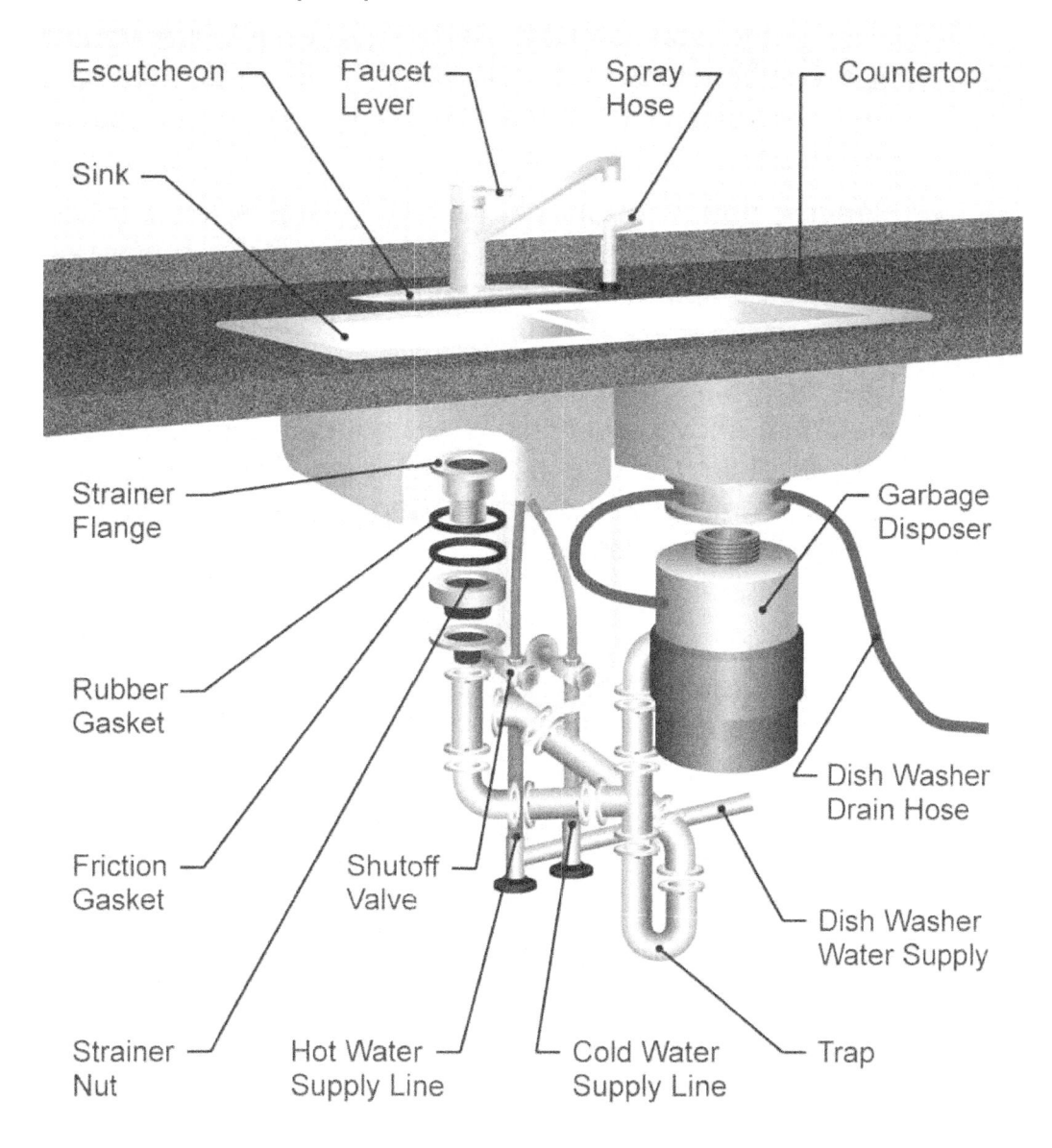

Dealing with a leaky sink can be stressful because your floors will always be wet from the leaks. Luckily this is a problem you can fix by following a few steps listed below:

- Identify the leak source: Below every sink are various pipe combinations that drain water to your main drainage line. Most sinks leak at the nut strainer, gaskets, or supply line pipes.

- Replace any worn-out parts: If your sink is leaking from the area around the friction gasket, you have a worn-out part. Use a spanner to disassemble the parts and replace the worn-out parts with new ones.

- Seal or replace any broken pipes: As you can see from the photo above, many pipes are beneath the sink. If your leak is at any of the pipes, the pipe needs sealing or replacement. Use a plumber's tape to seal any holes in the pipe. However, if that doesn't work, replace the broken pipe.

- Reassemble everything back together and test: After repairing, reassemble all the parts and make sure every part is tight. Run water down the sink; you should see no leaks.

18. Fixing a Clogged Kitchen Sink

While any sink is prone to clogging, the kitchen sink is the biggest culprit, probably because it is the most used sink in a home. When you notice that water keeps flooding your sink, it is a clear sign that your sink is clogged.

Here are a few simple ways to fix the problem:

- Pour hot soapy water into the sink: Sometimes, the clog in your kitchen sink could be because you poured oily liquids down its drain. For example, if you were cleaning oily utensils on the sink, it could be that some of the oils froze and clogged your sink. Try melting away the fats by pouring hot soapy water, and watch your sink unclog in seconds.

- Clean using baking soda and vinegar: If hot soapy water does not do the trick, try using a mixture of baking soda and vinegar. This mixture is equivalent to the chemicals plumbers use to unclog sinks and pipes. Use a cup or any container to remove all the stagnant water from the sink. Pour about a cup of baking soda down your drain, making sure you push the powder down using a spoon if necessary. After that, pour one cup of white vinegar down the drain. Close the drain by putting a stopper to cover it. Give the mixture 15 minutes to do the magic. Remove the cap and flush the drain with hot water. This should unclog your sink.

- Use a plunger to unclog the sink: Another easy way to unclog any sink is to use a plunger. Simply place it at the draining hole while the sink has some water and plunge until it becomes unclogged.

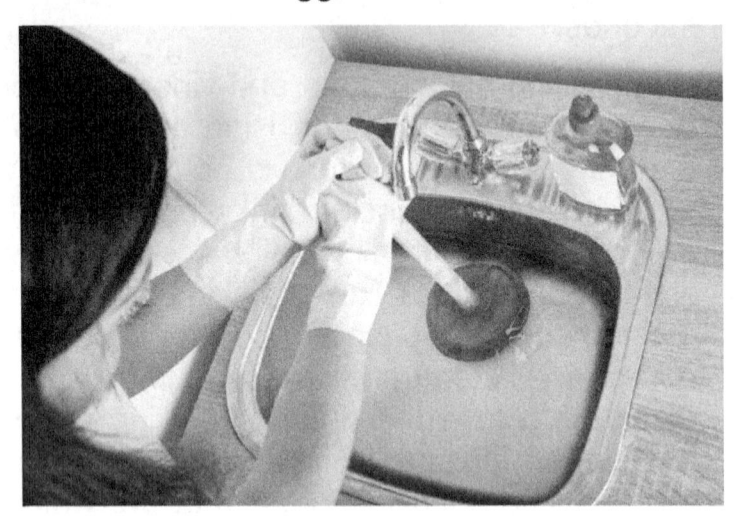

- Clean the P-trap: Do you see the elbow-shaped pipe underneath your kitchen sink? That is the p-trap. If the procedures above do not work and your sink is still clogged, your p-trap is probably the problem. You should clean it and remove any debris that could be causing the blockage. Simply twist the round part to open up the p-trap. Remember, it is bound to get messy; be armed with some towels, gloves, and goggles. In addition, place a bucket below the p-trap to ensure any water splashes into the bucket instead of the floor. After removing the p-trap, clean out any stuck debris and rinse it with clean water. Assemble everything back and enjoy your unclogged sink.

19. Repairing a Leaky Outdoor Faucet

Outdoor water faucets that leak are a nuisance, especially when it's hot outside and you need to replenish your swimming pool or run your handheld sprinkler. In addition, water leaks are expensive in the long run, so it's critical to repair any problems with your outdoor water faucets as soon as possible. Fortunately, most tiny leaks are easy to repair, even for beginners. Simply follow the steps below:

- Start by cutting off the water supply: Before repairing the outdoor faucet, remember to turn off the water supply completely. Otherwise, be prepared to get soaked. You will typically find the faucet shutdown valve in the utility room, crawl area, or basement.

- See if the packing nut is loose and tighten it: After turning off the water, go outside and unhook the hose from your backyard water faucet. You should find the packing nut beneath the faucet's handle. This nut is normally responsible for providing a watertight seal around the valve stem. A leaking water faucet can sometimes be because of a loose packing nut. If that's the case, tighten it properly using a wrench.

- Remove the valve and replace the washer if the leak is persistent: If the leak is persistent, remove the packing nut to access the valve and remove it. Often, all you need is a solid grasp and a little effort to pull it out. You can also take the faucet and the supplying pipe in your hands and turn them clockwise while dragging them upward. With a flat screwdriver, pry away the metal washer at the base of the lengthy valve stem. Then, replace that washer with a new one of the same size and reinstall the valve end. Put everything back together and switch the water back on to confirm if your faucet is fixed.

20. Fixing a Frozen Outdoor Faucet

A frozen outdoor water faucet can cause catastrophic plumbing issues. When a faucet freezes, it exerts a significant amount of pressure, which can cause spigot components to break and pipes to burst.

Luckily, with these few steps, you can save an outside faucet from a spring freeze:

- Open the faucet and wrap the handle with rags: After opening the faucet, wrap the handle, spindles, and supply pipe in old rags or napkins. Make the wrap as tight as possible, but allow enough space around the faucet opening for thawing water to flow freely.

- Pour hot water on the wrapped faucet to unfreeze it: Slowly pour water over the covered faucet. Soak the towels in hot water slowly, then stop and look for trickles coming from the faucet. It can take a few attempts before the spigot starts to unfreeze. Allow the water to flow for several minutes after you have a constant stream. Turn the tap off for a few seconds before turning it back on. Any frozen pipe parts behind the spigot should melt as water flows through the spigot. Repeat these two steps slowly to unfreeze your faucet.

Now that you know how to fix indoor and outdoor faucet issues, let's move on to drainage plumbing repairs.

Drainage Repairs for Tubs, Showers, Floor Drains, and More

As a homeowner, the last thing you should underestimate is the significance of drainage issues. While a clogged or sluggish drain may appear to be a minor issue, it may quickly become a major problem.

Slow drains can signal several issues, such as the early stages of a blockage, narrower pipes caused by mineral or fat accumulation, or even poor drainage system grading. Whatever the cause of the problem is, you need to fix it as soon as possible.

Let's look at how you can fix some of the most common drainage issues in a home.

21. How to Unblock a Clogged Shower/Tub Drain

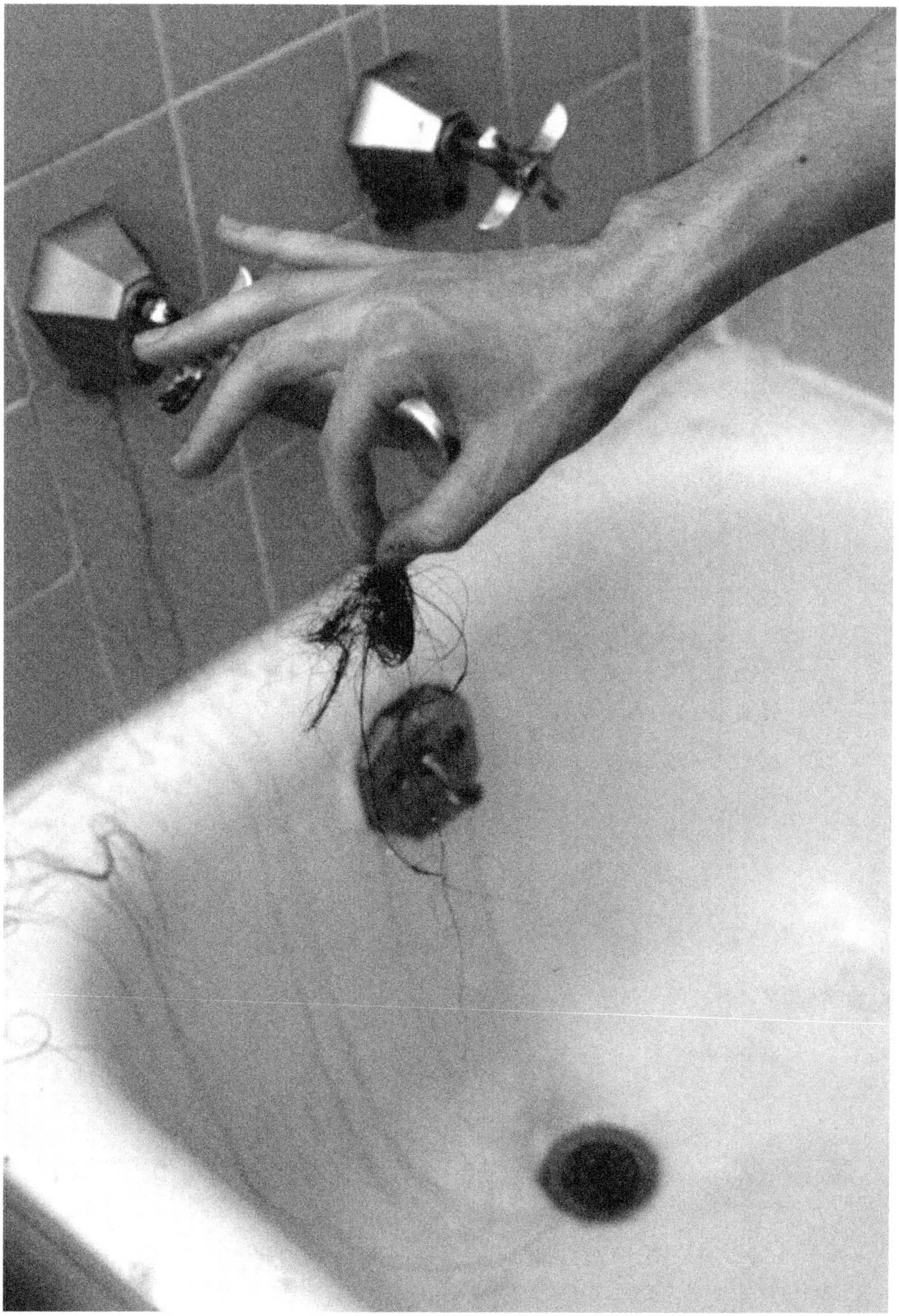

If you notice that water is not draining from your bathroom floor or the tub after a shower, your shower/tub drain is clogged. Follow the steps below to fix the problem:

- Pour unclogging chemicals down the drain: Sometimes, the clog is because of soapy particles and hairs that you can clear without opening up the drain. Buy an unclogging chemical from the hardware and pour it down your drain. Let it rest for 20 minutes, and then pour water. If the clog was nothing serious, your tub and bathroom floor should now drain with ease.
- Remove visible clogs by hand: A blockage can sometimes be seen at the top and is easy to reach. Put on a pair of latex gloves and try to remove the blockage as thoroughly as possible. Alternatively, you can use small plastic hooks to reach the clog. Although it may be alluring to use a coat hanger in this situation, be aware that doing so may cause damage to your drain.
- Use a drain snake for clogs too far down the drain: A drain snake or a plumber's snake is stretchy and

extendable drilling equipment available at hardware stores. You'll shoot a metal wire into your drain using the snake's hand crank to split up or pull out everything blocking it. There are also disposable plastic snakes available that don't require any cranking and can even be used to unclog a toilet. Remember to clean your drain snake every time you use it.

- Pour hot water down the drain: If there are no noticeable impediments obstructing the drain and using a plumber's snake hasn't worked, cleaning the drain with hot water can help disintegrate softer buildup from around the edges—like soap scum. Repeat the procedure two or three times more if necessary.

22. Repairing a Broken Underground Drainage Pipe

A broken drainage pipe in your lawn may not seem like a serious problem, but it is. It can cause flooding, contaminate the soil and water, and cause many health problems. Fortunately, fixing the problem is easy because all you need is to follow the steps below:

- Locate the pipe breakage and dig around that area: To begin, dig a hole in the earth to locate the broken pipe, which will most likely be near any visible damage symptoms, such as wet spots. Dig an extra six inches beneath the broken pipe place after locating the damaged pipe area to create a working space for yourself.

- Cut out the broken part: You'll need to cut out the broken region of the pipe to repair it. Measure two inches on either side of the broken spot and label the pipe before cutting. Labeling is important for accuracy purposes.

- Fix a new piece of pipe: Take measurements of the damaged pipe you removed before adding a new PVC pipe section to make sure the pipes blend in. The new pipe must have the same thickness as the old pipe to prevent leaking. After that, attach the new PVC pipe to the current pipe ends with flexible rubber connectors. Then slide the elastic connectors to cover both the old and new pipe sections.

- Confirm that there is no leakage and cover the ground: After replacing the broken part, let some water run through the drain to confirm no leaking. After that, shovel back the soil you had dug out to cover the hole.

23. How to Repair a Broken Shower Drain in a Concrete Slab

If you have an upstairs bathroom, the shower drain probably passes down behind your walls. If you notice wet patches on that part of the concrete wall, it could mean that the drain is broken.

Here is how to fix that problem:

- Remove the concrete around the drain: To dig out the concrete around the drain, you will need a hammer and a chisel. Dig out the concrete until you see the bolts and flanges holding the drain line against the wall.
- Unscrew the drain line from the wall and remove it: Using a wrench, remove the screws holding the drain line in place and remove the old broken drain
- Install a new drain: Replace the old drain with a new one. However, make sure that it is the same size to ensure it connects smoothly with the other drain parts. After that, test for leaks by pouring water into the bathroom drain.

- Put back new concrete

After fixing the new drain line and screwing it back to the wall, prepare new concrete and plaster it on the wall to cover the drain. Paint the new concrete to bring your wall back to its original look.

24. How to Fix a Smelly Floor Drain

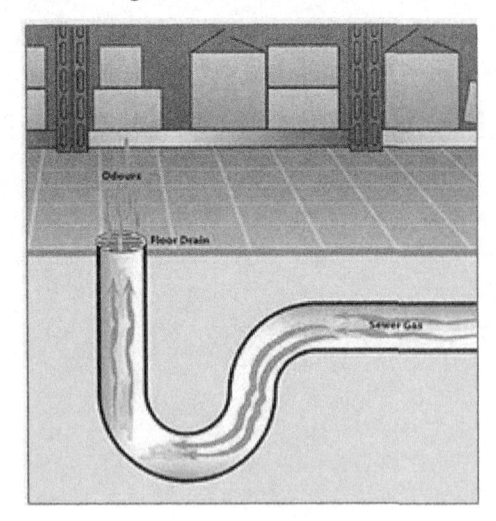

Most homes have floor drains in the bathroom, balcony, and other parts that need to drain water. Sometimes, you may notice a foul smell coming from the drain hole. To fix this issue, follow the steps below:

- Flush hot water down the drain: Sometimes, the stench from your floor drain results from oily debris clogged in the pipes. To wash this debris away, pour hot water into the drain.

- Pour a mixture of vinegar and baking soda down the drain: This trick works like unclogging kitchen pipes. The vinegar and baking soda dismantle all the clogs and eliminate the bad smell.

25. How to Repair a Leaky Plunger-type Drain on Your Tub

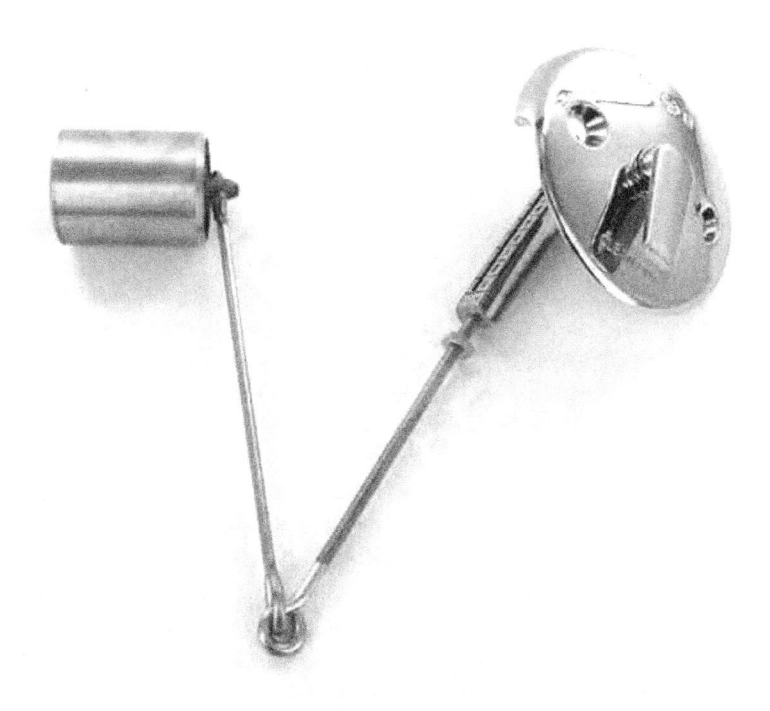

If your tub comes with a plunger, it most likely does not have a visible stopper. Instead, the plunger's lever pulls the hollow metal plunger down and up to seal the outlet. Therefore, if water seeps down the drain, the plunger is broken or clogged. If cleaning doesn't fix the problem, follow the steps below to replace the plunger and fix the problem:

- Extract the old plunger: Use a screwdriver to unplug the screw that secures the trip lever plate. Lift the linkages and metal plunger out of the overflowing drain by raising the trip lever plate. If the plunger does not connect to the linkage, insert a bendable grabber into the hole to extract it.

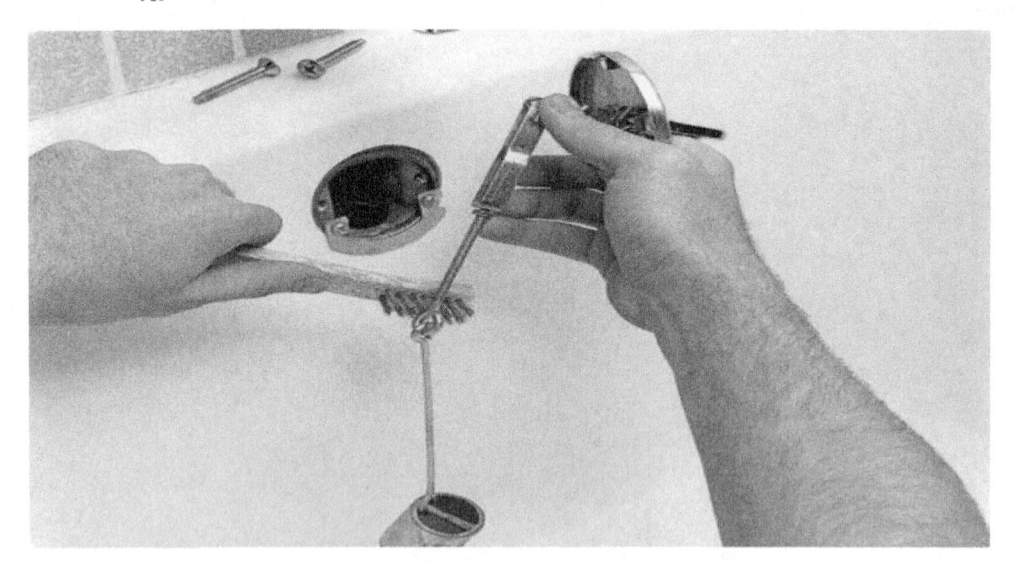

- Install a new plunger: Assemble the new plunger and install it in the same position as the old plunger. Screw it in place and test to see if water is still seeping through. If water seeps through, adjust the length of the linkage until it is tight enough to prevent water seepage.

I hope that by now, you can fix several drainage issues around your home. Let's move on and see how you can handle common piping problems.

Handling Pipe Repairs

You already know that pipes are a major part of your home's plumbing system —through pipes, clean water gets into your home, and the dirty water gets out. Given this, knowing how to repair different kinds of pipes around your home is a skill every homeowner should have.

Let's dive right in.

26. How to Repair a Leaky PVC Pipe Using Fiberglass Resin Cloth or Tape

If you notice a PVC pipe around your home is leaking, and you want a temporary solution, fiberglass resin tape is your best bet. Simply follow the steps below to seal the leak:

- Identify the leaking part pipe: Even though you may find water around the pipe, the chances are that the leak is only on a small part of the pipe. Dry the pipe and identify the exact area of the break.

- Place the tape on the broken part: Use a moist rag to clean the damaged section of the PVC pipe before applying the tape. Next, wrap the tape band around the broken area before the resin dries/cures then allow about 15 minutes for it to cure.

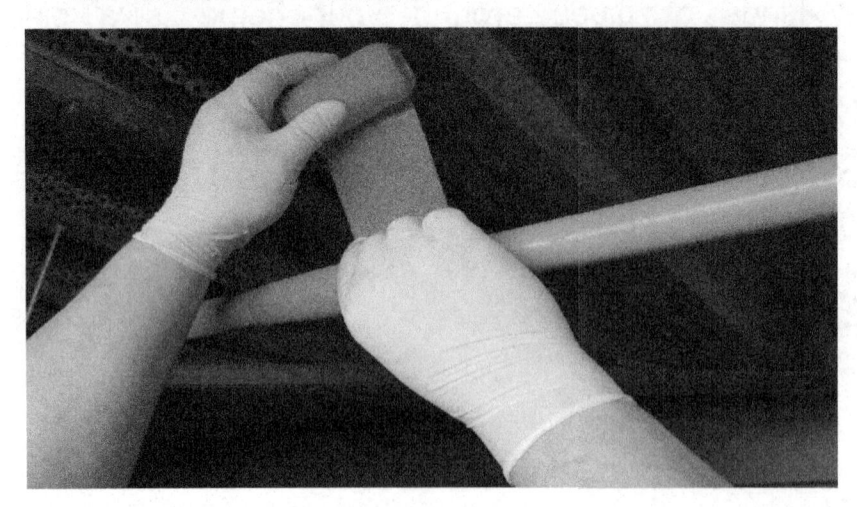

- Test to ensure there is no more leakage: After waiting for 15 minutes, the leakage should cease— the fiberglass tape inhibits the leakage by employing a water-activated glue, which usually hardens around the pipe.

- Alternatively, use a fiberglass resin cloth instead of tape: Replace the tape with a fiberglass resin cloth if you want a more permanent solution. First, clean the damaged part and use sandpaper to rub the area to make it more adhesive. After that, cover the damaged part using a resin cloth and put a UV lamp directly on the pipe or place the pipe piece under direct sunshine. This will cure the resin cloth and make it stick to the pipe eliminating the leak.

27. Repairing PVC Pipes Using Epoxy

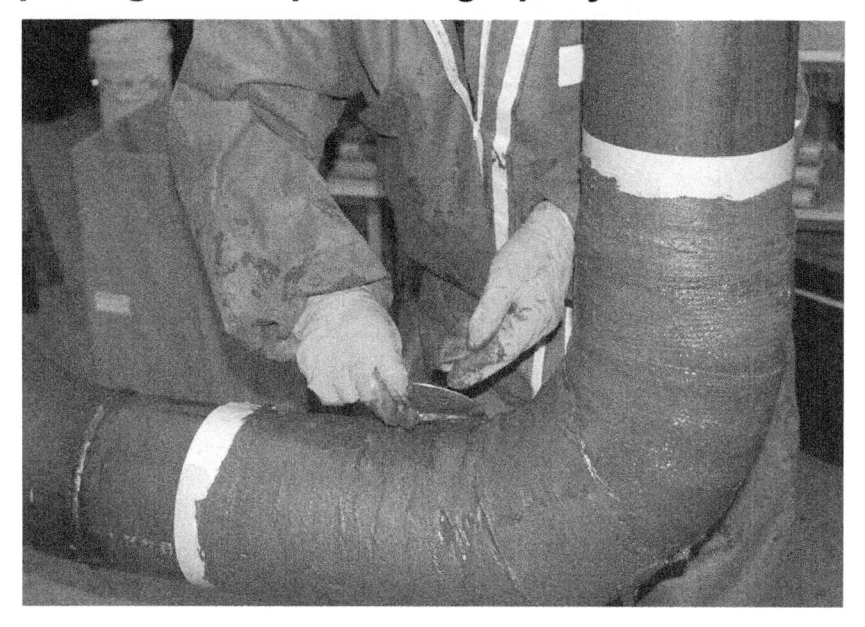

Another way to fix a leak on any PVC pipe without replacing it is to use epoxy using the steps below:

- Identify the leaking part: Epoxy is a repair fluid that hardens in minutes. To use, you must first identify all the leaky parts of a pipe before starting to apply the liquid. Wrap a dry towel around the areas you suspect to be broken and if the towel becomes wet, mark those areas with a bold pen.

- Turn off the water supply: After identifying all the broken parts, turn off the water supply. That way, you will have a dry pipe with which to work.

- Make the pipe surface rough: Because the smooth surface of PVC pipes makes adhesion problematic, you'll need to rough up the pipe with standard-sized sandpaper to ensure that the epoxy adheres properly. After sanding, use a clean, dry cloth to wipe away any dust.

- Mix the epoxy: Mix the epoxy components according to the ratio indicated by the manufacturer. These ratios differ from brand to brand; follow the manufacturer's guide. Remember to use gloves when mixing the epoxy components. More importantly, only mix epoxy that you can use in three minutes because it dries up very fast. Therefore, if you have several or many leaks to seal, you might need to repeat this mixing step severally.
- Apply the mixed epoxy: Wrap the final epoxy around your pipe in the marked spots. Make sure you press it on and expand it by at least an inch on all the broken parts.
- Let the epoxy cure and check for leaks: Although the epoxy plaster cures in approximately ten minutes, it takes about an hour to set fully. As a result, you should give it at least this long without turning on the water supply. Apply the hand towels test to the repaired parts to ensure that the fix has addressed any leaks. Although epoxy putty will provide a long-lasting repair, it's still advisable to check on it periodically afterward to ensure your repair worked.

28. How to Replace a Part of a PVC Pipe

Sometimes, a part of your pipe may be too broken to repair using epoxy or other materials. This leaves you with no choice but to replace the part of the severely damaged pipe. Follow the steps below to accomplish this task:

- Cut off the water supply first: Shut off the water supply first and let all the water drain away.

- Cut out the broken part of the PVC pipe: Use a hacksaw and cut out the broken part of the pipe. Measure at least 2 inches on both sides after the damaged part and make your cut there.

- Cut a piece of the new pipe and make it equal to the old one.: Cut a piece of PVC pipe the same diameter as the old pipe to the extent of the damaged portion. Use sandpaper to smoothen the ends of the new pipe and eliminate any burrs.

- Combine the old and new pipe: Spray PVC primer and cement on both the current and new pipe ends, and then connect the two with a coupler. Slide the edges of the new pipe into the existing pipe, then rotate the joints a little to disperse the mortar in between PVC joints. Give the repaired pipe 15-30 minutes to dry before using it.

- Turn on the water supply and check for leaks: After the primer and cement are dry, let water flow through the pipe and check for any leaks. If you measured everything perfectly, there should be zero leaks.

29. Repairing a Burst Metal Pipe Using a Pipe Patch Kit

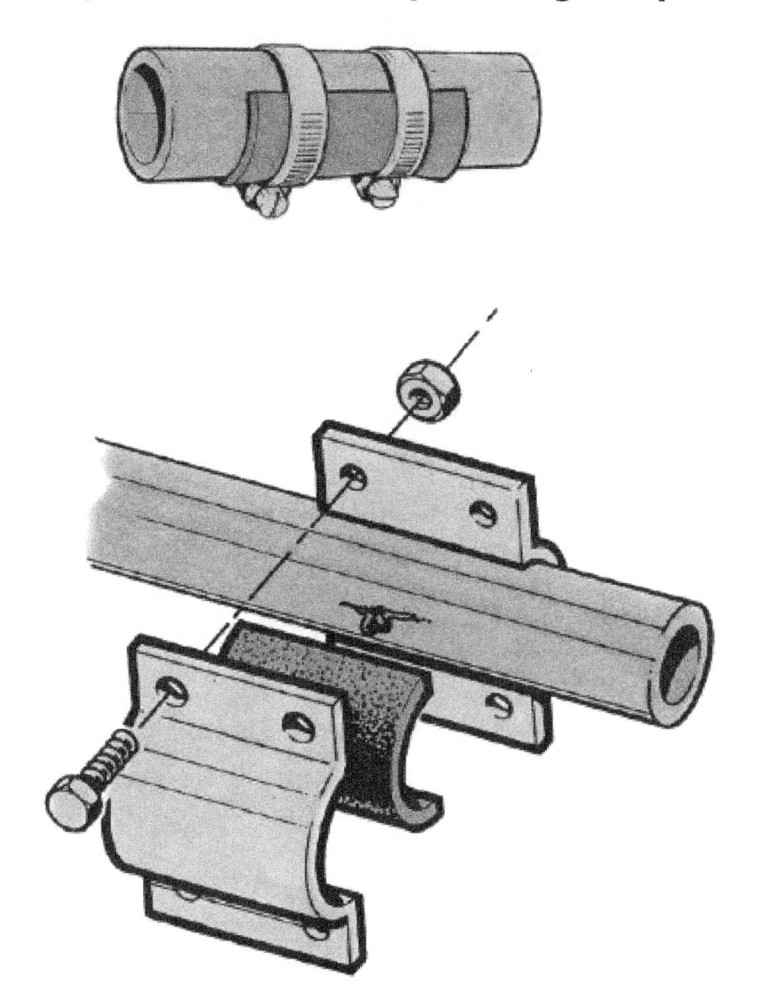

Having a burst metal pipe around your home can be stressful because it often means you need to replace it, which may be costly —after all, you will need to buy a new pipe. However, as you prepare to replace the pipe, you can repair it using a pipe patch kit to prevent further leaks. That way, your property will not suffer from water damage. Simply follow the steps below:

- Turn off the water supply: You can do this at the main water switch. In addition, open all faucets above the pipe to eliminate any water left in the pipe system.

- Inspect and dry the leaking area: Take a clean rag and wipe the burst area of the pipe. Scrub the outside of the pipe with steel wool if there is any lime or rust scale, then examine the source of the leak. If a pipe junction is leaking, use an adjustable wrench to adjust the joint fitting until it is tight enough. After that, mark all the broken parts of the pipe.

- Place a patch on all the broken parts: Cut rubber patches that fit the different leaking parts and place them on the surface of the pipe. Ensure the patches are at least one inch bigger than the broken part. Use a hose clamp to attach the patches and make sure the set screws of the hose clamp are firm in place by using a screwdriver to fasten them.

- Test for leaks: After patching all the leaky parts, turn on the water supply and confirm that there are no leaks.

30. How to Repair Leaky Pipe Joints using Silicone Caulk

Most of the time, pipe leaks will happen at the joints where one pipe and another connect. To fix such leaks, caulk the pipes by following the steps below:

- Purchase a tube of silicone caulk at the nearest hardware store: When making your purchase, make sure you ask for silicone caulk, not latex or acrylic caulk. Silicone is more water-resistant and durable than the others.

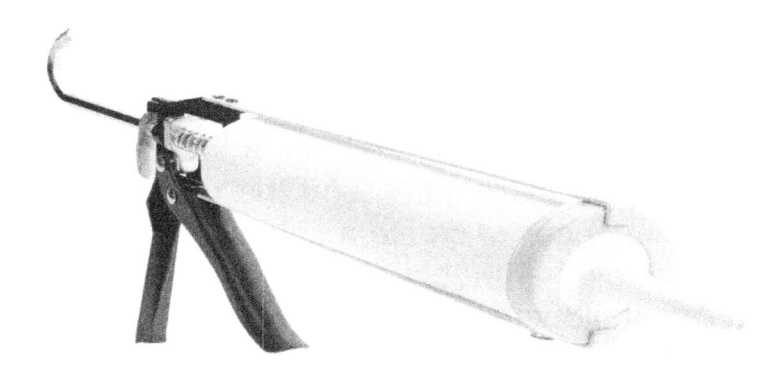

- Clean the pipe area that needs caulking after turning off the water supply: After turning off the water supply, use water, soap, and sandpaper to clean the surface of the pipe. Scrub the pipe until you eliminate all the dirt, filth, or debris. If you—or someone else—has caulked the pipe in the past, get rid of the old caulking. When the surface is totally clean, use a cloth to dry the pipe.

- Apply the Caulk: Use a razor or utility knife to cut the tip of the caulk tube. Make sure you cut the tip at a 45-degree angle. Place the tube in the caulk gun and start applying the caulk to the pipe using the slanted tip. Apply the caulk all around the pipe to ensure you leave no space at the joint.

- Smoothen the caulk and let it dry: After generously applying the caulk all around the pipe joint, smoothen it with your finger to create a tight seal and let it dry for an hour. After that, you can turn on your water supply to confirm that there are no more leaks.

Conclusion

I'm having a hard time putting into words how much your support and readership mean to me as I sit down to compose this. Writing is an intensely private and frequently lonesome activity, and only when there is a link between author and reader does the written word truly come to life.

I could not have foreseen the amazing encounters and connections that my job would introduce into my life when I first started on this journey. Every review, every comment, every email, and every communication I get from readers like you serve as a reminder of the value of narrative storytelling and the pleasure that comes from reading.

Your choice to read and buy my book has profoundly moved me, and I am honored and thankful for your help. I hope my writing has in some small way been enjoyable, enlightening, or inspiring—possibly even all three! Writing is a skill that demands equal amounts of discipline, creativity, and vulnerability, and it can only survive thanks to the kind support of readers like you.

I sincerely hope that, in some small way, my book has had a beneficial influence on your life. I am thankful for the chance to have shared this experience with you, whether it has taken you to a different time and place, changed your perspective, or has just given you a few hours of amusement and escape.

Please know that your comments and reviews are greatly appreciated by me, and I consider them as I work to improve my writing and find my unique style. I value your ideas and viewpoints, and I'm determined to use them to become a better writer.

I'd like to end by expressing my sincere appreciation for your support and reading. I will always be grateful to you for giving me the opportunity to share my enthusiasm with the world. I hope that reading my novel has made your day better and that it will stay with you for the ensuing days and weeks.

heartfelt respects,

Belle Hudson

Printed in Great Britain
by Amazon